Finding Comfort

by Marie B. Jackson-Peoples

RoseDog Books
PITTSBURGH, PENNSYLVANIA 15238

RoseDog Books
585 Alpha Drive, Suite 103
Pittsburgh, PA 15238
Visit our website at www.rosedogbookstore.com

ISBN: 979-8-88812-455-0
eISBN: 979-8-88812-955-5

Finding Comfort

Finding Comfort

Given today's climate, how to find comfort: Follow the rules of life. Do what is expected of you; be a leader. Prayerfully make clear and good decisions that may be difficult at times; however, that's a part of life's journey. Adhere to the rules that generate success/happiness, and you will have peace of mind. Learn to experience the peace of comfort, and demonstrate this behavior as you walk through life. Others will see how tranquility and happiness bring everlasting peace and contentment during a lifetime.

Grief

Acute sorrow is too costly to be wasted. Distress should be put to good use. If the energy of mourning can create some positive change, there can be a feeling that the loss was not in vain. If the lost of mourning can be translated into a spiritual awakening that we all must experience drama in this life sooner or later, we should have the belief that there is a higher being who will envelop positive change, and there will be a feeling that the suffering and loss was not in vain.

When we mourn over sin, no kind of grief holds more promise. Sometimes, we are broken over sin that we find in ourselves or in someone we love. This is the suffering that Jesus had in mind when He said, "Blessed are those who mourn for they shall be comforted."

In scripture, Paul realized that sin is worth crying over! We shed many tears over loved ones. God's Word says, "…but that you might know the love which I have so abundantly for you."

The God Almighty sends His spirit and His people to comfort, encourage, and support those who have experienced this kind of sorrow that change hearts.

When God brings us to our knees in weakness, we must accept this downtime as part of His great plan for our lives. Have a little talk with Jesus! He's waiting!

Comfort must not be seen as a byproduct of suffering/Christ. It is preparation for us to comfort and encourage others who suffer. The Holy Spirit used Paul to this awareness of the "God of all comfort." It shows a comfort that is found when we learn to rely on God rather than ourselves. It was in weakness that Paul learned to rely on the Lord and to take heart from God's ability to rescue him from the shadow of death.

Only when we are brought to the end of ourselves are we in a positive position to see more of God than we have seen. Trouble does not always come to the godless. A lover of God can be stripped of strength. A faithful follower of Christ can go through unbearable physical agony, such as deep anguish of the soul and a lack of personal peace before coming to the awareness of how completely and wonderfully God can comfort.

For the followers of Christ, there is no crown of comfort without a cross of suffering.

Hard times reveal our need of God in ways that good times do not. That's one reason God doesn't exempt Christians from suffering in this sin-cursed world. We must learn to accept pain, weakness, and despair as Christians' growth. Don't feel guilty because we experience strong sensations of weakness and incompetence. We allow our trouble to do its painful work in bringing us to God. For the person who lets his problems drive him to dependence on the Lord, bountiful comfort is on the way. You don't have to see it to believe it is coming.

Being right with God puts us in a position of strength. Trust and obey His Word. Let Him bear your burdens for you. Believe in the Lord Jesus Christ. The Scriptures assure us that He will forgive anyone who believes in Him. As you travel through life, confess your wrongs to those you have hurt. Assure them that you are no longer attempting to deny or cover up your wrongdoing.

Don't do this for the forgiveness and mercy of the other person. Admit your wrongs before God. It is the right thing to do. Discover in the Lord, our God; the strength that can be found in His forgiveness but also the comfort of a good conscience.

For the person who lets his problems drive him to dependence on the Lord, bountiful comfort is on the way. You don't have to see it to believe it, it is coming!

Find Comfort in Songs

Despite the lack of surprise, however, each time we listen to a favorite song, we relisten again and again. We explore extremes by relistening. The deepness in the connection to the song, draws you back.

How much did you hear the first, second, or third time? How did it make you feel the first time? Depending on the situation while listening, even when you listen three or more times, did it affect your mood?

Songs can make you feel happy, calm, angry, or even bittersweet. After approaching several people whose favorite song made them feel happy, they reported being drawn back because of soothing lyrics, rhythm, or beats. People whose favorite song made them feel bittersweet reported having a deeper connection to the song than those whose favorite evoked other feelings. These patterns held irrespective of music training. In difficult times, many folks rely on music for strength. The more times people listened to their favorite song, the more the song listeners can hear internally.

Oftentimes, when a song is heard over and over again, each time, something new is heard. People enjoy the background instruments, which gives prominence to the song's melody, beat, rhythm, or lyrics. Many songs help listeners find comfort when they are faced with difficult situations in their lives. The right song can change the listener's mood and his/her entire demeanor. Often, the beat or rhythm was especially important for relistening. In fact, the more times persons listen to a song, the more of it they could hear in their heads.

There is a song that makes you teary-eyed or emotional almost every time you hear it. You wonder why it is so stirring, so you ask yourself, when did this song become one of your favorites and why?

Make your own list of comforting songs. I believe music can be a unifying force for generations to come. Music can provide universal soothing for our souls. We could call it a rare form of communication, which will bond our souls forever. Songs reminds us that we are not alone in our struggles. Someone or something has paved the road ahead.

Music is good for one's soul. Different types of music help us remember that others need our comfort and support as we bridge the gap to what lies beyond our imagination and future. It's good to have a go-to song when you need to feel something special in your life. If your life had a theme song, what would it be?

Find Comfort in Sorrow

*Let not your heart be troubled, you believe in God, believe
also in me. In my father's house are many mansions; if it
were not so, I wouldn't have told you. I go and prepare a
place for you, I will come again and receive you unto myself;
that where I am, there you may be also, And, where I go—
you know the way... I am the way, the truth and the life.*

When God brings us to our knees in sorrow and weakness, we
must accept that downtime as part of His plan to strengthen us
for the trials ahead as we travel through life. In God's consoling
Word, it shows a comfort that is found only when we learn to rely
on Him rather than ourselves.

Hard times reveal our need of God in ways that good times
do not. That's one reason God doesn't exempt Christians from
suffering in this sin-cursed world. Sometimes, we must let trouble
run its course. While doing so, don't feel guilty because we experience strong sensations or weaknesses, foolishness and incom-

petence. Let's not be misled about the comfort of God. A person who lets his problems drive his/her dependence on the Lord, bountiful blessings are on his/her way to help ease the pain. A good conscience and comforting feelings will help encouraging roles of the Holy Spirit to go together.

Note: The Spirit will not bring to our hearts the reassurance peace of God's presence if we are violating our conscience. Be aware! Nothing will rob us of the consolation and help from the Comforter of our souls more than an unresolved sense of guilt.

Believe in the Lord Jesus Christ. The scriptures assure us that He will forgive anyone who believes in Him. Claim His promise!

1 John 1:9:

*If we confess our sins, He is faithful and just to forgive us
our sins and cleanse us from all unrighteousness.*

Sorrow that change! Sorrow must be put to good use. That's true whether we are mourning the loss of a loved one, a loss of health, or any other tragic reversal. If the energy of mourning can be translated into some positive change, there can be a feeling that the suffering and loss was not in vain.

Find Comfort in Being Alone

Enjoy living today, tomorrow, and every day for the rest of your life. No matter where relationships will begin or end. Some examples! Loss of a spouse, child, loss of a job, a failed business, or loss of one's home may cause a person to withdraw, to mention a few. We are reminded that each person's loss or suffering has its own unique quality. No outsider can fully enter into it.

As we move through life, we leave behind familiar waters we'll never sail again. The carefree days of childhood; the feel of a doll or a new truck; hitting your first home run; excitement of a first kiss; the sounds of a first car; the pet you grew up with; the joy of bringing children into the world; and more. When we leave these things behind, it hurts to say goodbye. Sooner or later in this life, the things we hold dear are taken out of our hands forever.

Now, who comforts us in all our tribulations that we may be able to recognize others when comfort is needed? We look to God for this comfort. God has a special interest in consoling those who are willing to join Christ in suffering on the behalf of others. All who are in Christ need to die to our own self-interest, so that the powerful life and love of God can flow through us. This is not an easy task. It is not a matter of doing what comes naturally. It's supernatural as we choose to join Christ.

However, this approach to comfort may involve discomfort. Personal efforts in intercessory prayer in the discipline of letter writing and visiting the lonely sometimes involve a difficult and painful process. We must expose ourselves to the risk and discomfort of suffering with Christ. We will never know the fullness of His comfort until we experience the reassuring love of God; we will not be able to pass that encouragement along to others. The more we share God's love and comfort with others, the more we will experience God's love and comfort in our own lives. Remember, downtime with God is part of His plan. When He brings us to our knees in weakness, we must accept that time as part of His work in our life. Don't let self pity and pre-occupation with tribal thinking make things worse. Some people need to understand that comfort must not be seen as an end in itself. It is to be seen as a byproduct of suffering with Christ and a preparation for equipping us to comfort and encourage others who suffer.

Find Comfort in Weakness

Find in a place, spiritual solace and consolation through the Holy Spirit. This comfort is found only when we bring awareness to our own weakness by conquering our deficiencies through Christ.

For we do not want to be ignorant of our trouble, which came to us in Asia. We were burdened beyond measure, above strength, so that we despaired even of life. We had the sentence of death in ourselves, that we should not trust in ourselves but in God, who raises the dead, who delivered us from so great a death, and does deliver us; in whom we trust that He will still deliver us.

A lover of God can be stripped of strength. A faithful follower of Christ can go through almost unbearable physical agony, deep anguish of the soul, and lack of personal peace before coming to the awareness of how completely and wonderfully God can comfort.

The Bible teaches us through Paul that we do not want to be ignorant of our trouble. Just as there is no winner without competition; no victor without a war; no wages without work, there is no crown of comfort without a cross of suffering. Note: Trouble provides an environment for growth. Paul learned that when we have the sentence of death in ourselves, it is so that we should not trust in ourselves, but in God, who raises the dead. Let's not be misled about the comfort of God. As in Paul's case, it may be preceded by devastatingly difficult experiences, yet it's wonderful to know that in God's time, comfort eventually comes to the person who puts his weakness to work for God. When you are driven to the Lord, bountiful comfort is on the way.

When God brings us to our knees in weakness, we should accept this downtime as part of His plan for us. According to Paul (2 Corinthians 1:8-11) scriptures:

> *For we do not want to be ignorant brethren of our trouble which came to us in Asia: that we were burdened beyond measure, above strength, so that we despaired even of life. Yes, we had the sentence of death in ourselves that we should not trust in ourselves, but in God who raises the dead that He will still deliver us. No matter the circumstance(s), nothing is too big for our Lord and Savior, Jesus Christ.*

Winning coaches tell their teams as they prepare to win: "No pain, no gain." Our Lord knows something similar; without something to expose our weakness, we would get confused without circumstances that reveal our own need of the Lord. We would settle for a life full of ourselves, rather than a life full of Him.

Difficult times reveal our need of God in ways that good times do not. That's one reason God does not exempt Christians from suffering in sin. Therefore, to work together with His purposes, we must, at times, let trouble run its course. Do not resist and deny what is beyond our ability to control; we must learn to accept pain, weakness, and even despair as seasonal winters of Christian growth. When experiencing strong sensations of weakness and incompetence, we should not feel guilty. Our God is always there!

Find Comfort in Discomfort

A great day is coming when God will forever vanquish all loss.

God will wipe away every tear from their eyes. There shall be no more death, nor sorrow, no crying. There shall be no more pain for the former things have passed away.

That will be a glorious day of restoration when our relationship with God and our relationship with other people who have died in Christ will be restored. Never again will we have to say goodbye. Every believer hopes for that day. Allow yourself the freedom to enjoy life again. The joy of the Lord is not something we control. It is the product of the pursuit of God through obedient living and is produced by the spirit. Joy will catch us by surprise; when it does, enjoy it. Begin filling your spiritual album with photos of joyful times. The spirit gives you these to keep when the days are bleak. Your zeal for Christ's return would not have been possible had you not walked through the life changing valley of grief. "We know that God has all things under His control." It is okay to grieve. Some of us are uncomfortable with the mourner's feelings. We spend too much time insulating ourselves from pain. When confronted with someone's raw grief, we try to keep our own pain to a minimum. Don't try to distract mourners from grief to avoid your own discomfort. This can only prolong the mourning. This kind of comfort does more harm than good. Many people who attend church regularly seem just as uncomfortable with grief as the rest of society. The church should be different because of the hope of restoration we all share in Christ. As missionaries of the gospel of reconciliation, we have entrusted with the privileged opportunity of being in the presence of Christ with those who are grieving. Words are inadequate to express what the individual griever needs. It is the shoulder to cry on, listening and having the commitment to sit in silence that communicate the most. We all feel uncomfortable with some situations where we can do nothing. Your presence is something! It tells the person who is grieving that you are willing to walk with the grieving person along this painful path that one must travel. The last thing they need is to feel abandoned by others around them. They need true friends who will listen, not only with their ears, but with their hearts. Those persons who will reach out with the love and the comfort of Christ are needed. Volunteers sometimes graciously make meals, babysit, continue to pray and provide support, which is essential for recovery from a loss.

We are never far from the pain of those we have lost! Death does not have the final say. A great day is coming when God will forever vanquish all loss. There will be no more pain. A glorious day of restoration, when our relationship with God and our relationship with others who have died in Christ will be perfectly restored, never to say goodbye again. That is the hope of every believer who grieves over loss.

Find Comfort in Death

During our walk through the valley of grief, we can cling to this simple yet profoundly secure truth: "Jesus loves me, this I know, for the Bible tells me so."

Heaven is the habitation of God. It is also the place where His saints will dwell forever: "Our Eternal Home." Death involves physical and spiritual separation, not annihilation. Physical death occurs when the soul is separated from the body. The believer in Christ may die physically, having his soul separated from his body. However, he can never die spiritually. He will never experience the separation of his soul from God. In John 5:24, it states, "He who hears my word and believes in Him who sent me has everlasting life." When you die in Christ, you enter into the presence of God. Jesus comforted Martha that her brother would rise again. A beautifully stated truth:

I am the resurrection and the life. He who believes in me though he may die, shall live. And whoever lives and believes in me shall never die.

We believe beyond all doubt in the existence of a glorious city called "the Heavenly Jerusalem." This heavenly city, planned and built by God, is mentioned in Hebrews 12:

> *But you have come to Mount Zion and to the city of the living God, the heavenly Jerusalem to an innumerable company of angels.*

In the new Jerusalem, a river of crystal will flow forever, reminding us for all eternity that God has graciously and abundantly provided for our every spiritual need. Here, the New Jerusalem will be the tree of life, which refers to a species. There will be many trees. God's Home will be the home of blessedness. We will have a new heaven and a new earth. In John, his vision recorded his vision of an immense city of shimmering beauty, descending slowly from heaven to become the capital city of our eternal home. This city will be eternal abode of all who have placed their faith in Jesus Christ. In our eternal home, we will join the saints of all the ages in a spirit of communion, fellowship, and love…all centered on Jesus Christ. Our sins will be removed, and we will understand the blessings and glory of our life in heaven.

Who or what can be with us? We will discover there is a safe place to rest. People who can hear God say, "I will never leave you nor forsake you," then you can say, "The Lord is my helper, I will not fear when we learn the meaning of this truth." We will discover that even if others abandon us, or die on us, we will not only survive but will prosper. Learning to have faith in God will allow us to not only survive, but we'll prosper. Learning to have faith in God will not exempt us from the sting of loss, but will provide us with the resources we need to deal effectively with grief. It will free us to love again. While knowing the meaning of sadness and disappointment, we are yet able to remain joyfully alive.

Find Comfort in the Spirit

The Word of God offers comfort only as it leads us to the spirit of Christ. Do you need comfort? Pray in cooperation with the Spirit of the Lord. Read and analyze the Word in a way that will help you come to a new dependence on the Spirit. Faith plays an enabling role in your life. The God of all comfort, we must trust God's eyes rather than our own. In 2 Corinthian 4:13-18:

> *But since we have the same spirit of faith according to what is written, I believed and therefore speak, knowing that He who raised up the Lord Jesus will also raise up [fix]. ... For all things are for your sakes that grace having spread through the many which may cause thanksgiving to abound to the glory of God. Therefore, we do not lose heart. Even though our outward man is perishing. Yet, the inward man is being renewed day by day. For our light affliction, which is but for a moment is working for us far more exceeding and eternal weight of glory, which are not seen. For the things which are seen are temporary, but the things which are not seen are eternal.*

God wants us to admit that it makes sense to trust the God who raised Christ from the dead more than it does for us to trust the appearance of our ever changing circumstances. Note: The Spirit who empowers: We are sufficient of ourselves to think of anything as being from ourselves, but our sufficiency is from God, who made us sufficient as ministers of the New Covenant, not of the letter, but of the Spirit; for the letter kills, but the Spirit gives life… Now, the Lord is the Spirit, and where the Spirit of the Lord is, there is liberty. But we all, with unveiled faces, beholding as in a mirror the glory of the Lord is being transformed into the same image from glory to glory. The reality is that when losing a loved one, you will not get over the loss, you will learn to live with it. You will heal, and you will rebuild yourself around the loss you have suffered. You will be whole again, with the help of the Holy Spirit, but you will never be the person you once were.

Find Comfort in Foods

Comfort foods are expensive and difficult to make are contradictions. Our grandparents went without the basic nutritional foods. There were certain foods that grew naturally from the earth. During the fifties, many vegetables grew without cultivation. The earth was rich with nutrients during those years. Meals were created by experiments. Measurements weren't used, you tasted as you created new meals which were passed on to friends and family members. Grocery stores, in rural areas, mainly made their money on flour, seasonings, corn meal, lard, sugar, fat back meat from hogs and vegetable that were grown in the area. A lot of intuitive recipes from one or more countries in Africa expanded heavy foods that we later called comfort/soul foods. Women experimented and relied on their taste buds. Most of them during the thirties, forties, and even fifties worked hard over wood stoves, constantly putting in the wood/coals into cooking stoves to keep the top and the inside oven hot enough to cook foods.

Women during the twenties or earlier relied on intuitive recipes that were stored in their memory banks because many could not read or write. Older relatives and also close friends shared these dishes by word of mouth. They stood over hot stoves to produce the slowest-simmered sauces that could season many kinds of meats. Routinely, leftover meats from dinner/supper reappeared on the breakfast table with scrambled eggs the next day. Food was never thrown away.

For many people, comfort foods at home are a way of reconnecting, or maybe connecting for the first time. These high calorie foods, if kept/preserved in moderation, can be stretched for several days. Soul foods go a long way when it comes to keeping cravings under control.

Comfort foods are great for obvious reasons, so never feel bad or guilty about indulging once in a while. Enjoy in moderation. It's also helpful to find other coping methods for stress, like meditation/exercise or a little extra self care. These foods provide a sentimental value, especially to rural life. Note: Many people were reared in the south on farms or plantations. High calorie foods were the way of life, but somehow, obesity was not a problem. These foods are great for obvious reasons, so never feel bad or guilty about over indulging once in a while. Enjoy!

Find Comfort in the Person Who Cares

I am filled with comfort. I am exceedingly joyful in all our tribulations. For when we came to Macedonia, our flesh had not rested, but we were troubled on every side. Outside were conflicts, inside were fears. Nevertheless, God who comforts the downcast, comforted us by the coming of Titus, and not only by his coming, but also by the consolation with which he was comforted in you, when he told us of your earnest desire, your mourning, your zeal for me, so that I rejoiced even more.

God comforts through people. We can see that the help and consolation of the Holy Spirit often comes through our brothers and sisters in Christ. The scriptures bear this out as we are called on to comfort and encourage one another. The comfort of the Spirt may not seem mystical. But in many ways, it is. Those who commit themselves to a role of encouraging others will often sense that they are not doing this work of comfort on their own. Often, they will sense that it is actually God comforting others through them. Seek to know God on His terms. Desire to join Him in loving others. Learn to see life as He wants you to. But even when you've done all this, don't expect to merit anything along the way. All the comfort we can hope for is that comfort we don't deserve. Yet praise the LORD, it is the comfort we don't deserve that the Lord delights to give to those who are broken and humbled before him.

> *Let not your heart be troubled—you believe in God. In my father's house are many mansions. If it were not so, I would have told you. I go to prepare a place for you. And if I go and prepare a place for you. I will come again and receive you to myself, that where I am, there you may be also. And where I go you know the way, the truth and the life. No one comes to the Father except through me.*

The Holy Spirit of God comes alongside us to comfort, strengthen, and reassure. We have seen that He is with us not to reinforce our own ways, but to strengthen and comfort us in the way of God.

Put yourself at the mercy of Jesus Christ. Trust Him to be the only one who will lead you to the Father and to the kind of comfort in this life and the next, that only He can give.

Find Comfort in the Strength that Sustains

Grace is the undeserved favor and help of God. It is that undeserved help that is received by those who have been broken enough to bend the knees of their heart before God. This is the undeserved help in which Paul found so much comfort.

> *And lest I should be exalted above measure by the abundance of the revelations, a thorn in the flesh was given to me, a messenger of Satan to buffet me, lest I be exalted above measure. Concerning this I pleaded ... with the Lord three times that it might depart from me. And He said to me, "My grace is sufficient for you, for my strength is made perfect in weakness." Therefore, most gladly I will rather boast in my infirmities that the power of Christ may rest upon me. (2 Cor. 1:7-10)*

The Lord knows what we are made of, even if we don't know. What effect did this have on Paul in the Bible)? Whether he was temporarily devastated or not, we don't know, but he came out at the right place. He came out affirming that grace, what he didn't deserve, was all the comfort he needed. Seek to know God on His terms. Desire to join Him in loving others. Learn to see life as He wants you to. But even when you've done all of this, don't expect to merit anything as you travel through life. Note: All the comfort we can hope for is that comfort we don't deserve. Yet, we should praise the Lord: It is the comfort we don't deserve that the Lord delights to give to those who are broken and humbled before Him.

The Holy Spirit of God comes alongside us to comfort, strengthen, and reassure. We have seen that He is with us not to reinforce our own ways but to strengthen and comfort us in the ways of our Lord. Note: The Holy Spirit does not begin with minds focused on the Spirit of God Himself. Inner strength comes as we focus our attention on the Lord Jesus Christ. This comfort comes as we listen to the One who sent the Spirit.

Let not your heart be troubled; you believe in God, believe also in Me. In My Father's house are many mansions; if it were not so, I would have told you. I go to prepare a place for you. I will come again and receive you to Myself; that where I am, there you may be also. And where I go you know, and the way you know ... I am the way, the truth, and the life. No one comes to the Father except through Me. Say yes to Him.

Have you done that? Do you recognize your own sin and unworthiness to approach the Father in your own way? If you're not sure, continue to read Romans, the third chapter. Then, in the awareness of your own spiritual bankruptcy, put yourself at the mercy of Christ. Trust Him to be your Savior from sin. Trust Him to be the only One who will lead you to the Father and to the kind of comfort, in this life and the next, that only He can give.

We all face different challenges throughout our days here on Earth; and we all can look to Jesus moment by moment for help, strength, and peace. He will help us to hold back from snapping at our loved ones; He will give us the courage to do the next hard thing. Look to Him and find contentment.

Share your Comfort with Others

One purpose of dealing with discomfort is to invest into the lives of others who need the same comfort that comforted us. That is true of our calling as people who are created in the image of God: to love God and to love others. Discomfort reminds us that this world is not our home; that we are just passing through.

> *To believe in Christ's rising and death's dying is also to live with the power and the challenge to rise up now from the dark side of discomfort.*

If sympathy for the world's wounds are not enlarged by our disappointment, if love for those around us is not expanded, if gratitude for what is good does not flame up, if insight is not deepened, if commitment to what is important is not strengthened, if aching for a new day is not intensified, if hope is weakened and faith diminished, if the experiences are unfavorable, then the discomfort has won.

We all feel uncomfortable with situations where we can do nothing for those who are in trouble. Remember, you can't change what has happened. What the person wants to know, but does not ask is:

Will you walk with me along this painful path that I must travel?

They feel abandoned. The last thing they need is to feel abandoned by others around them. They need true friends who will listen not only with their ears, but with their hearts; those who will reach out with the love and comfort of Christ.

Practical support in little things is needed. Things like taking a meal to someone in need; cleaning a home for a disabled person; financial management; and continued prayer support are essential for recovery.

We can comfort those in any trouble with the comfort we ourselves receive from God. Our Father comforts us, and when we've experienced His comfort, we're enabled to comfort others. Our compassionate Savior, who suffered for us, is more than able to comfort us in our suffering and distress. He helps us through our pain and equips us to do the same for others.

Comfort Stories to Share

One: Lend a Hand!

The next month will be very difficult for many people who are still reeling from a loss this past year. The crippling hurt caused by the absence of a loved one can cloud holiday gatherings and even dim the desires of celebrating Jesus's birth.

In a poem written by Ann Weems:

> *Some of us walk into Advent tethered to our unresolved yesterdays, the pain still stabbing, the hurt still throbbing. It's not that we don't know better; it's just that we can't stand up any more by ourselves. On the way to Bethlehem, will you give us a hand?*

In the Bible, Paul gives ways to express practical Christianity in our relationships. One seems needed at this time of year: Rejoice with those who rejoice, and weep with those who weep.

We can "give a hand" to grieving friends and family by understanding their sorrow and not expecting them to "get over it" in time to celebrate the holidays. We can freely mention the name of the person whose death has brought such desolation and then share a fond memory. We can be quiet, listen, and pray for God's help. Only God can heal the deep wounds of the heart, but we can lend a hand.

> *If I can help some wounded heart,*
> *If I can by my love impart*
> *Some blessing that will help more now*
> *Lord, just show me how!*

Two: Newgrange!

Newgrange is a 5,000-year-old burial passage tomb in Ireland. Built by the members of a farming community in Ireland's Boyne Valley, this magnificent structure covers more than an acre of land. It was a place where people went to struggle with the issue of death. It is best known for the beam of sunlight that moves through the chamber for 17 minutes each day from December 19 to 23 during the winter solstice, the shortest days of the year. Some say it serves as a powerful symbol of the victory of life over death.

Ever since death entered the human experience in Genesis 3, it has been life's one great inevitability, and many people's chief fear. It need not be so, however. The apostle Paul wrote:

> *For if by the one man's offense death reigned through the*
> *one, much more—those who receive abundance of grace and*
> *of the gift of righteousness will reign in life through the one,*
> *Jesus Christ.*

From that moment in the Garden of Eden with the sin of our first parents, sin and death reigned. Yet we need not fear death or its consequences. Because of Christ, we can have confident hope—His victory of life over death has given us eternal life.

Three: Learning to Comfort!

Blessed be the God and Father of our Lord Jesus Christ, the Father of mercies and God of all comfort.

When she heard that her best friend's baby died, Andra didn't know what to do. Should she call her friend right away or wait a few days? What should she say? She asked her mother, Mary, a children's hospital chaplain, for advice.

"Phone her now," her mother said. "Tell her you love her and that you'll call back later."

Andra followed that advice, and it meant a great deal to her friend.

How should we respond when those we care about suffer a loss? Second Corinthians 1:4 tells us that God "comforts us in all our tribulations, that we may be able to comfort those who are in any trouble, with the comfort with which we ourselves are comforted by God." It's in God's school of comfort that we learn to better understand the needs of those who hurt. Mary Farr writes:

We live in a fragile and imperfect world tinged by broken-ness and cloaked in unanswered questions. Some things truly aren't fair. This is hard.

She encourages people to resist the temptation to fill the silence with talk. Instead, we need to be comfortable with saying. "I don't know," and not try to provide easy answers. And when there's nothing to say, just sit together.

The comfort God has given us, He wants us now to share
with others who are suffering and caught in life's despair.

Find Comfort in Songs

The Negro National Anthem

Lift every voice and sing,
Till earth and heaven ring.
Ring with the harmonies of Liberty;
Let our rejoicing rise High as the listen skies,
Let it resound loud as the rolling sea. Sing a song full of
the faith that the dark past has taught us,
Sing a song full of the hope that the present has brought us.
Facing the rising sun of our new day begun,
Let us march on till victory is won.

Stony the road we trod,
Bitter the chastening rod,
Felt in the days when hope unborn had died;
Yet with a steady beat,
Have not our weary feet.
Come to the place for which our fathers sighed.
We have come over a way that with tears have been watered.
We have come, treading our path through the blood of

the slaughtered,
Out from the gloomy past,
Till now we stand at last,
Where the white gleam of our bright star is cast.

God of our weary years, God of our silent tears,
Thou who has brought us thus far on the way;
Thou who has by Thy might
Led us into the light,
Keep us forever in the path, we pray. Lest our feet stray
from the places, Our God, where we met thee;
Lest, our hearts drunk with the wine of the world, we for-
get Thee;
Shadowed beneath Thy hand, May we forever stand.
True to our God,
True to our native land.

The Star-Spangled Banner

O say can you see, by the dawn's early light.
What so proudly we hail'd at the twilight's last gleaming.
Whose broad stripes and bright stars through the perilous fight.
O'er the ramparts we watch'd were so gallantly steaming?
And the rocket's red glare, the bombs bursting in air,
Gave proof through the night that our flag was still there,
O say does that star-spangled banner yet wave
O'ver the land of the free and the home of the brave?

On the shore dimly seen through the mists of the deep
Where the foe's haughty host in dread silence reposed,
What is that which the breeze, o'er the towering steep,
As it fitfully blows, half conceals, half discloses?
Now it catches the gleam of the morning's first beam,
In full glory reflected now shines in the stream,

'Tis the star-spangled banner—O long may it wave
O'er the land of the free and the home of the brave!

And where is that band who so vauntingly swore,
That the havoc of war and the battle's confusion
A home and a Country should leave us no more?
Their Blood has wash'd out their foul footstep's pollution.
No refuge could save the hireling and grave,
And the star-spangled banner in triumph doth wave
O'er the land of the free and the home of the brave.

O thus be it ever when freemen shall stand
Between their lov'd home and the war's desolation!
Blest with vict'ry and peace may the heaven rescued land
Praise the power that hath make and preserv'd us a nation!
Then conquer we must, when our cause it is just,
And this be our motto—"In God is our trust,"
And the star-spangled banner in triumph shall wave
O'er the land of the free and the home of the brave.

America (My Country, 'Tis of Thee)

My country tis of thee,
Sweet land of Liberty
Of thee I sing:
Land where my fathers died,
Land of the pilgrim's pride,
From every mountainside,
Let freedom ring.

My native country, thee,
Land of the noble free

Thy name I love:
I love thy rocks and rills,

Thy wood and temple hills,
My heart will rapture thrills,
Like that above.

Let music swell the breeze
And ring from all the trees,
Sweet freedom's song:
Let mortal tongues awake,
Let all that breathe partake,
Let rocks their silence break,
The sound prolong.

Our Father God to Thee,
Author of liberty,
To Thee I sing
My country 'tis of Thee,
Sweet land of liberty,
For all eternity
Let freedom ring,
Let freedom ring.
My country 'tis, my country 'tis of thee

*Be Kind

It doesn't hurt to be kind,
Just try it and you will see.
Pleasant days will be yours,
And happy you will be.
It doesn't hurt to be kind.
Do try it if you please.
You will make a better life;
You will be at ease
It doesn't hurt to be kind,
Just give yourself a chance.
Others will be kind to you;
Your life will be enhanced.

*We Do Not Say Goodbye

We do not say goodbye who come to mourn.
The tears we cry are really not for you.
We are the lonely, we are sad, forlorn,
For when you died a part of us died too.
It is for us the living to endure
The aching pain your passing left behind;
Your happiness is finally secure,
You have the peace which none of us can find.
The reason you were chosen can't be known.
We would have kept you longer if we could,
But God called you unto His very own.
He surely must have thought that you were Good,
While missing you will make life incomplete,
The memory of your presence will not die,
And since some happy day again we'll meet,
As you proceed, we do not say goodbye.

*Thanksgiving

We thank thee for thy blessings,
That flow throughout the years,
The rainfall and the sunshine,
That give us happy tears.
We thank thee for the good things,
That makes all men free;
The days of joy and of peace.

That come to us from thee.
We thank thee for thy grace,
The things for which thou stand;
Thy strength, thy comfort and love
That come from thy great hand.

Understand Your Physical Grief

Exercise Daily

A good walk will relax you physically and soothe your frayed nerves. Daily walks help me to escape from the pain I feel while in my home. To be outside in the fresh air, surrounded by God's creation, lifted my thoughts to Him. The exercise made me feel refreshed and ready for the day.

Take a Relaxing Bath or Shower Before Bed

Water is a wonderful healing agent. It soothes and relaxes tired muscles and joints. Hot tubs and jacuzzi are wonderful sources of relaxation, but be careful not to stay in longer than 15 or 20 minutes.

Eat a Healthy Diet

A diet high in fresh fruits, whole grains, fresh vegetables, and low in fat, protein and sugar is best for your health.

Daily Exposure to the Sunshine

The warmth of 15 minutes a day of sunshine (when available) is soothing to the nerves.

Lots of Fresh Air

Deep breathing exercises will increase oxygen that is needed for mental clarity. Slow, rhythmic breathing that uses the abdominal muscles for inhaling and exhaling will act as a tranquilizer, relaxing all muscles of the body.

Daily Exercise

Try to walk, jog, or garden. You will accomplish numbers 2 or 3 and 4 all at one time.

Stay Away from Substances that Will Hinder You

Examples of these are alcohol, tobacco, drugs, sugar and sweets.

Abundant Internal and External Use of Water

Drink a minimum of eight glasses of water each day.

Regular Rest and a Good Night's Sleep

A routine will be the key to achieving success.

Trust in God

He alone is able to bring you peace.

Comfort Examined Biblically

People who suffer from physical or emotional illness need understanding and sometimes loving confrontation, but never criticism. Once in a while, God touches our hearts and minds with circumstances such as sickness, joblessness, or family problems to get our attention. These situations only bring stress and discomfort. Being critical of a situation only brings more stress.

The Book of Job in the Bible demonstrates how God used Job to show his faithfulness. Therefore, God used Him to show his faithfulness to the world. He was removed from a place of comfort into a situation of stress and pain. For a time, Job's body was covered with loathsome boils. He suffered miserably. At the same time, he was grieving for the loss of his children and his wife had turned against him. His friends believed that all these calamities were punishment for something he had done. Many Christians today believe that you reap what you sow.

Job looked in vain for someone to comfort him. This well-known story carried a solemn admonition to every Christian:

People should not openly judge a person's character because he or she has not been afflicted with this kind of unknown disease. So, what is your point! Walk into another man's shoes before you judge!

Many of us, Godly or ungodly, have endured suffering. It's not our job/duty to tell them whether or not God is chastening them. Our part is to help bear the load. Suffering people need our words of comfort, not criticism.

> *Give me a heart that is touched by those who sorrow and are distressed; Give me a heart of sympathy ... For the burdened and depressed are unlimited, so train your heart to give sympathy and your hand to give consolation with comfort.*

Lastly, comfort is that space in our heart which brings contentment. Commit yourself to all of the beauties in this world. Test everything and hold on to that which is good. We should not to be governed by the way something looks, feels, or sounds. Instead, seek your inner self for wisdom and strength to do what is correct. Don't repeat your mistakes. Take time to reflect on past achievements. Ask yourself what motivated you! Consider your lifestyle and set realistic goals.